Printed in the United States of America

Typography by Brian R. Kinney

Printed by
Penmor Lithographers,
Lewiston, Maine 04240

Published in 2012 by
American Hot Rod Foundation
P.O. Box 372
Cos Cob, CT 06807-0372, USA

The information in this book is true
and complete to the best of our
knowledge. All recommendations are
made without any guarantee on the
part of the author or Publisher, who
also disclaim any liability incurred
in connection with the use of this
information and advice.

We recognize, further, that some
words, model names, and
designations mentioned herein are
the property of the trademark
holder. We use them for
identification purposes only. This
is not an official publication.

Library of Congress Cataloging-
in-Publication Data:

The Great American HOT ROD
Explained / M. deLesseps, Author.
ISBN 978-0-9823477-1-3
(hardbound w/ jacket)
1. Hot Rods – United States History.
I. deLesseps, M.

Library of Congress Catalog Card
Number 2012910641.

The Great American
HOT ROD
Explained

The American
Hot Rod Foundation

M. deLesseps

Foreword

Nowadays, it seems that we have a lot of young people who know little about cars or other mechanisms. What happened to high school shop where you learned to fix and modify cars? I'm afraid our focus on academics squeezed it out of the curriculum. And since this has been going on for quite a while, it seems we have a lot of adults who also know little about cars! The problem with all this is that knowing how to fix and modify a car is a necessary security blanket in this complex world. It's a basic skill set that offers comfort and enjoyment.

Almost from the beginning of the American Hot Rod Foundation in 2002, we thought about publishing a book on hot rodding that would explain to kids and adults what this great hobby is all about. I imagined it would be a magical book. It would slow down the reader from today's warp speed, go back in time, and experience hot rods and hot rodding for what it was then – fun, adventure, camaraderie, and common sense. But who could write such a special book, and since it would be magical, who could illustrate it?

I knew that my friend, Michael deLesseps, was a long-time hot rodder. But when I saw his two books on pond models, I knew he was the author/illustrator who could realize our dream. You see, Mike is a big kid. Yes, he's been a top advertising Art Director, won Clio's, "did it all", but the kid never left him. He enjoys life thoroughly, tackles projects with glee, wonders aloud at even simple things, breaks any rules that get in his way, and just has that Maine sense of what's important and what's not.

As you read Michael's interesting text, and enjoy his beautiful watercolor illustrations, I know you'll agree with me that this is the right way to tell the magical tale of hot rodding. I've turned these pages many times already and I'll be back again and often. No matter what your age and familiarity with hot rodding, this book is for you. And if you happen to be a little kid or a big kid, all the better.

Steve Memishian

It all had to start somewhere...

Once upon a time there was
an enterprising gent who
simply wanted his car
to be faster than the others.
The first HotRod.

What is a HotRod?

We have tried for years to answer the question, "what is a HotRod?" The simple fact of the matter is, if you ask five hundred people what a HotRod is you will get more than that many different answers, even if you ask hardcore HotRodders.

Every one in the hobby today has his or her definition of what a HotRod is. To settle the issue we have tried to define the term once and for all:

The name HotRod is not a Definition it is a Concept.

To create the answer as best we can, we have defined it here and then put the dictionary to work to clarify our meaning. The two words Definition and Concept are defined below.

def.i.ni.tion: 1, an act of determining; specific, a word or phrase expressing the essential nature of an activity or thing. 2, a statement of the precise meaning of a word or a sign or symbol.

con.cept: 1, something conceived in the mind, thought or notion. 2, an abstract idea generalized from particular instances. Syn. see idea, an idea or thought.

You really should decide for yourself, it's your choice.

The great American HotRod had to start sometime, exactly when is history and since none of us were there then all history is an invention. Based on what few facts remain it would be impossible to say exactly what the first HotRod was and what it looked like, all lost in the past.

Rather than invent we speculate based on what remains. It is safe to say that the first HotRod was a roadster or a coupe. The enterprising soul who built it had one thing in mind: Speed.

The first HotRod was probably a Model T with the engine modified or altered to get as much power as could be squeezed out of it. Lots of back yard ingenuity was needed to get any real performance out of the first crude engines.

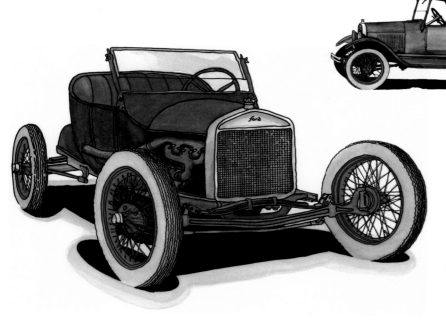

The late Model T Ford roadster was very sedate until it got lowered and stripped of non-essentials like fenders and splash pans and some serious speed equipment added.

Since the engine is a very important part of a HotRod we will start with how they work and a little about their early HotRod development. There are a number of different engine designs, the most popular for cars is called the four stroke and no matter how many pistons and cylinders there are they all work the same.

The four strokes are easy to understand if you think of the piston traveling up and down in the cylinder in a specific order. **One, Intake** The intake valve opens as the piston travels down into the cylinder drawing in a mixture of fuel and air. **Two, Compression** The piston having reached the bottom of the cylinder the intake valve closes and the piston travels up

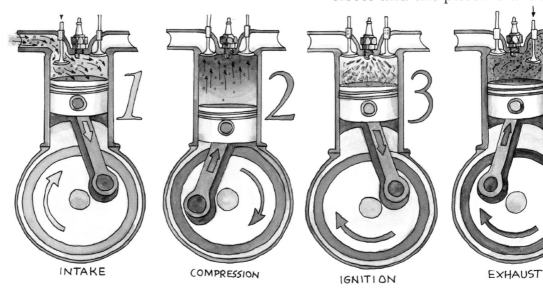

INTAKE   COMPRESSION   IGNITION   EXHAUST

The pistons are moving up and down in the cylinders on connecting rods which rotate on the crankshaft and each cylinder is a tightly sealed compartment with valves on top to control the movement of air, fuel and exhaust in a cycle of four strokes.

compressing or squeezing the fuel and air charge. **Three, Ignition** The piston having reached the top of its travel has squeezed or compressed the fuel and air mix and the spark plug fires igniting the mixture forcing the piston down with considerable force. Ignition or power stroke.

4

Four, Exhaust The exhaust valve opens as the piston travels back up the cylinder pushing the spent and burned gasses out the exhaust. All those exhaust strokes releasing the burned gas produce a wonderful sound. This sound is an important part of the HotRod experience, that wonderful rumble of combustion.

This order happens thousands of times, with the pistons going up and down each doing its part as the engine is running.

A very important part of that four stroke action is tied to other parts that keep everything in order. Look at the engine drawing below to identify those other parts. The pistons each have a rod that ties it to the crankshaft so when it rotates they are free to move up and down.

The brains of any engine is the cam which is a shaft with a series of bumps or lobes on it which is moved by a gear on the crank. The crank gear turns the cam and it opens and closes the

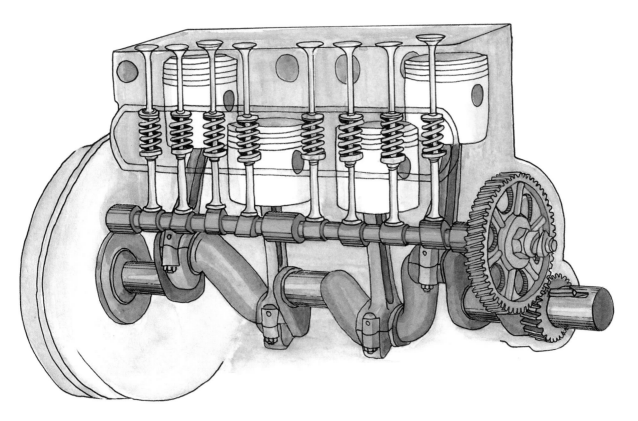

valves, timing the opening and closing of the intake and exhaust valves to keep the strokes moving in the right order as the pistons require it. The importance of the camshaft cannot be emphasized enough. When the valves open and shut is critical to performance, ask any knowledgeable Hot Rodder. Referred to earlier as the engine's brain, the bumps' or lobes' shape is critical to what the engine will produce for power. The cam lobes open and close the valves as the crank rotates and pistons move up and down.

Exactly when the valves open and how long they stay open and close is how the engine breathes. One might ask why this breathing is so important to engine performance?

This lobe with its very sharp point is going to open and shut the valve very quickly as it rotates, open/close not giving the cylinder much time to get a good charge of fuel... the next lobe shows an altered shape leaving a flat spot on top to hold the valve open a little longer, allowing a bigger charge of fuel, this is called duration.

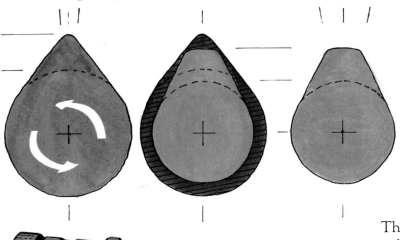

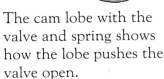

The cam lobe with the valve and spring shows how the lobe pushes the valve open.

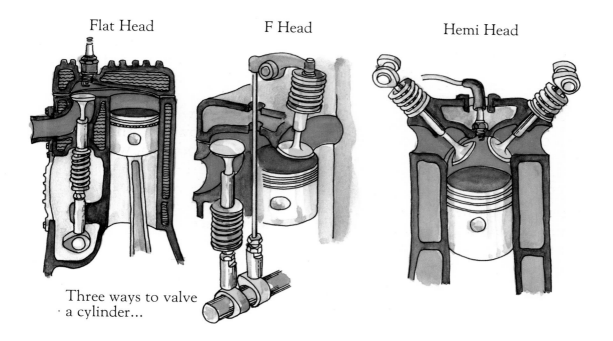

Flat Head   F Head   Hemi Head

Three ways to valve
a cylinder...

When the piston moves up and down in the cylinder the cam opens the valve and it draws in a charge of fuel and air, the more fuel and air the engine can draw in, burn and expel, the more power it will make. Look at the shape of the first cam lobe. As it pushes the valve open you can see the cam simply opens and shuts the valves by the way the cam face or ramp is designed, open, shut. Look at the other lobes and notice the face is much flatter on top holding the valve open longer, this is called duration. With a wider face the valve will be open longer letting in and letting out more fuel/air and exhaust giving a lot more power. The last drawing on the left is the valve assembly for a flat head engine. Called a poppet valve, the spring keeps the valve shut until the cam opens it. As the cam lobe passes the valve the spring snaps it shut.

The basic idea of what is called a reciprocating engine aka: a four stroke, didn't change much in all the years they have been made but where the valves and camshaft were put in the engine radically developed and changed. As the fuel/air delivery flow improved through the engine the power increased as well.

7

HotRod Ford/Mercury
flat head early version
1932-1948.

Dual carburetor manifold with fuel pump and fuel lines

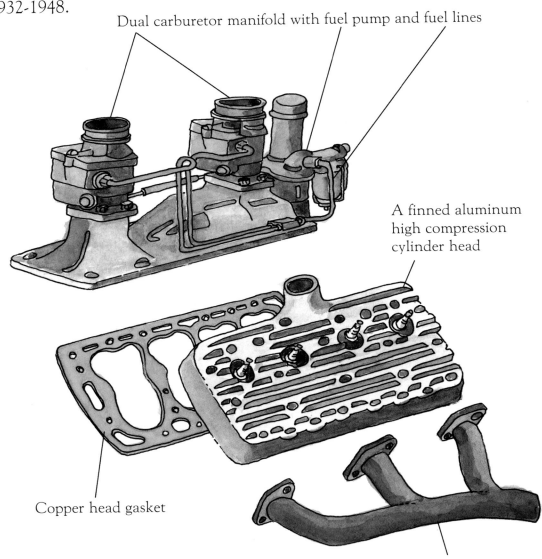

A finned aluminum
high compression
cylinder head

Copper head gasket

The three joined
pipes are headers
for spent exhaust
gases

The earliest engines manufactured for cars had the right idea. They were a simple design that had all the basic parts, they were cheap to manufacture and they worked. Over the years all those same elements inside the engine got re-arranged and put in different places producing today's modern engines.

The first engines were called flat heads. They got that name because the head on the engine was nothing but a flat panel with passages in it for cooling and a convenient place to put the spark plugs, right on top of the pistons. If the head was removed from the block what is seen is the four cylinders with the pistons in them. What one would also see on that flat surface is a row of valves, two for each cylinder, one intake and one exhaust.

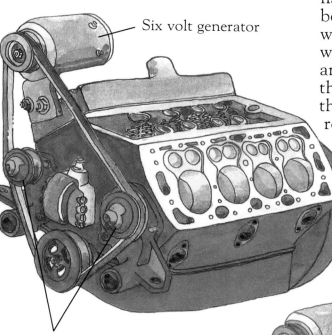

Six volt generator

Water pumps

Divers helmet front mounted type distributor.

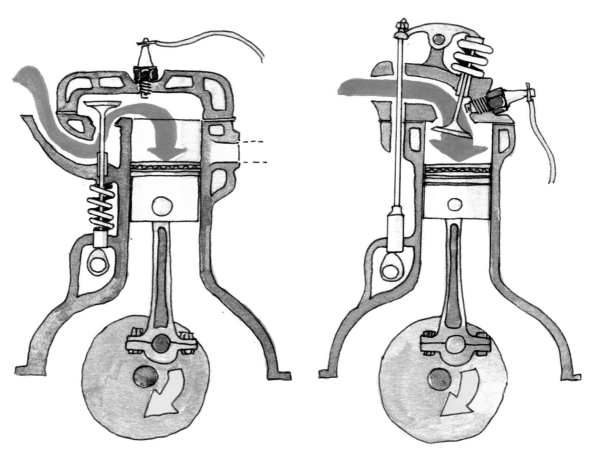

Flat Head   Overhead Valve

Getting an engine to breathe efficiently given the structure is very difficult. The red flow arrows show why it is important for performance. Look at the flow or movement of the fuel and air mixture (in red...) past the valves on top of the cylinders.

The most direct passage, the straight line is always going to be the most efficient. On an early flat head engine the fuel mixture starts straight down into the engine, turns back up and passes thru the open valve and then has to turn completely back on itself to travel down into the cylinder. With the valves in the head on top the mixture simply goes in an almost straight line from intake to piston to exhaust making a huge difference in performance.

The flathead T engine did not have an oil pump. The oil dippers on the connecting rods forced oil up into the engine as they rotated on the crank. The valves were in the engine block so it didn't breathe at all well. The carburetor was crude and the ignition was a strange array of coils in a box that fired the spark plugs. Buried inside the engine was a magneto to produce the electricity needed for the ignition.

It had a two speed planetary transmission and if the Hot-Rodder wanted to get a better top speed he would have found a two speed rear axle.

The planetary gear box is operated by three pedals that gave it only low and high gear. Neutral was found on one pedal half way down, down all the way was low and out all the way was high. With the pedal half way down in neutral one could then push reverse to back up, the third pedal was a brake. Note that the Ts only had brakes on the rear two wheels. As crude as the Model T engine

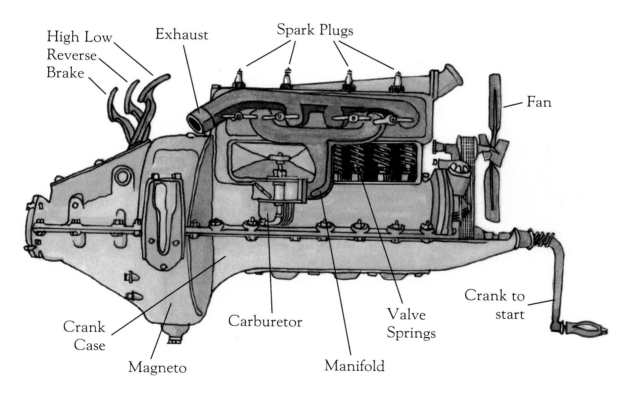

High Low
Reverse
Brake

Exhaust

Spark Plugs

Fan

Crank
Case

Magneto

Carburetor

Manifold

Valve
Springs

Crank to
start

A modification available for
the Model T in 1925.

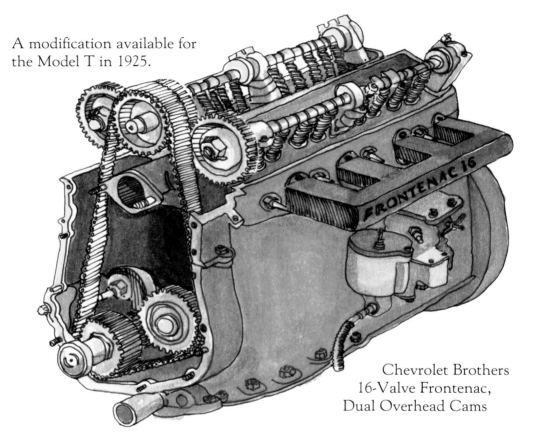

Chevrolet Brothers
16-Valve Frontenac,
Dual Overhead Cams

was it had a long history of HotRod and race activity. Even after the early V8 engines were introduced, the Ford Model A and Model B 4-cylinder engines continued to be heavily modified and raced, and won many events at time trials and in racing. That engine had many years head start in development and was hard to beat, especially with an overhead valve arrangement bolted to the top.

Before we leave the four cylinder engine to its place in history a comment or two regarding the development of the overhead valve fours. In 1925 the Chevrolet Brothers offered an OHV head called the Frontenac. It was a truly amazing development offering dual overhead cams driving 16 valves, four on each of the four cylinders, a total of 16. This and other offerings from specialty manufacturers kept the fours competitive for years after the V8s were introduced. But it was only a matter of time.

With the new V8 engine getting the attention of the HotRod bunch it didn't take long for those extra four cylinders to have a big effect. As the V8 became more powerful it found its way into a lot of Model T and A roadsters and coupes, leaving the venerable T engine in the dust of time.

We have covered the fours, the earliest years, when Hot Rodding was populated by really hard core guys looking for speed, an edge over the other engaged in the same pursuit. Performance gains in the four cylinder years were hard to come by and expensive.

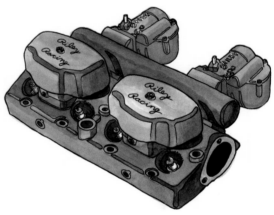

The Model T & A Fords were raced for many years and accumulated an enviable record, none of which could have been achieved without the specialty performance parts manufacturers like Craig-Hunt, Rajo, Riley, and Cragar.

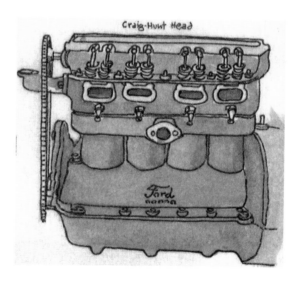

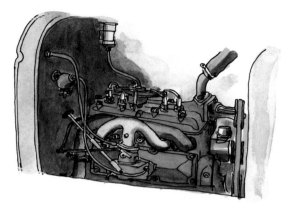 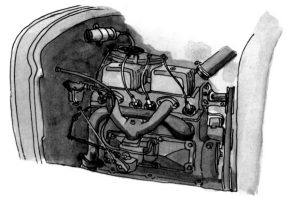

Even modified the new Model A Ford
was losing ground to the new V8.

With the introduction of the early Ford flathead V8s in 1932 there were a lot of cheap cars and engines, many of the best could be found abandoned in backyards and junk yards. Well, they call them salvage or recycling yards now but back in the 30s it was a junk yard where little money could get everything needed to build a car, a HotRod.

It's not hard to imagine a kid with his first driver's license going to high school everyday and working a part time job to make a few bucks. Prowling the neighborhood and the junk yards looking for the material to build his first car. There are wonderful first car stories of abandoned roadsters or coupes found in a field, dragged home and rebuilt, even better tales of roadsters bought and towed home only to have Dad say no... take it back. The late twenties and early thirties must have been a great time to have come of age, Southern California was the place. No wonder the whole concept of the HotRod happened. By that time American manufacturers had made a lot of automobiles and there were a fair amount of worn out and bent or twisted examples in every community, in back yards and otherwise available cheap. Just what an enterprising youth was looking for. Pieces, parts here and there and lots of help from his friends, a little shade tree ingenuity and

STREET RACE

before long a running auto, wheels, freedom and with some luck and more hard work and tinkering a roadster that could run with the best of them. It was all about speed. And, there were enough of them to promote impromptu street races in broad daylight at stop signs or clandestinely arranged night contests on roads out of town off the beaten track. The authorities took a dim view of these activities and it wasn't long before clubs were formed followed by the SCTA (Southern California Timing Association) to channel that enthusiasm, to recognize the how shall we put it... the need for speed. As it happened one of the great areas of America for hard core speed freaks is right above Los Angeles, places in the high desert called the Dry Lakes. A huge expanse of dried mud flats with little to run into

Time Trials. Dry Lakes

for miles. The SCTA set up timing traps and the racers came to run flat out and get a timing slip. Some cars were driven from home. Others were flat towed to the flats. It got the speeders off the streets and when successful a little plaque for the dash to prove your accomplishment. Pictures from that era show the dry lakes activities and the earliest Hot Rodders looking for speed. If you could get a record at any of the Dry Lakes or later on the Bonneville Salt Flats you had really accomplished something. Legions of guys put in years of hard work, plotting and scheming how to get the car a little lighter or finding where a few extra horses were hidden. Oh and windage, getting it

Pierson Brothers '34 Coupe

This is the quintessential Dry Lakes Coupe. One look tells it all, a radical arrangement that made many assaults on the speed records set on the flats.

   This might be the best example ever of a radically Chopped top, any lower than that and the driver would not be able to see out.

16

low and light without presenting too much frontal area. Ever put your hand out a car window traveling at sixty, you know what drag means. Probably for any high school student in those times it was simply the ability to get yourself and your friends around to the drive-in for a soda and a burger, freedom.

We will leave the opening engine section here with the fours while we have a look at some of the early cars built as HotRods, then we will return to the V8 engine era and the later overhead valve powered HotRods. Aside from the obvious refinements over the years the same basic structure is still built and driven today.

This small showing of early HotRod favorites only begins to tell the HotRod story. The possibilities are endless especially when you consider all the cars that haven't been rodded yet.

The model T Ford will always be with us, this one is a roadster otherwise known as a T-Bucket. They come in many different styles and have been powered by everything you could imagine from a little four banger to the biggest big block. The last T was built and sold back in 1927.

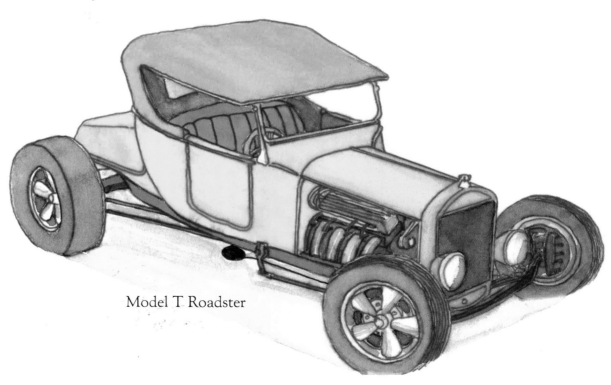

Model T Roadster

From 1928 to 1931 there was the
Model A, again by Ford. Model
A's were made in great numbers
and after a few years were very
affordable rod material. This
little pickup truck is a 1931 A
and you can bet that with that
big V8 it really scoots. Trucks
are fun and often useful.

Model A pickup with
a Deuce grille shell

Three very popular rods today, the Ford Deuce Roadster, the coupe and sedan, perhaps the most popular HotRods since the invention of the HotRod.

The Deuces have probably had every popular engine known stuffed into their respective chassis. The Deuce coupe is no slouch in that area as well.

The all time King of HotRods the Deuce or 32 Ford, everybody's favorite.

And just as useful and a great driver for family and friends the Deuce Tudor.

Here's an example of a chopped top, a modification very popular with Hot Rodders. You can see here how cutting some height out of the roof can really make a big difference in appearance.

Coupes come in three window and five window arrangements. Take a look and see if you can spot the difference.

Another of the timely greats in
early rodding is the 40 Ford
coupe, so popular in fact that
over seventy years after Ford
produced it there is a brand
new steel replica offered for sale.
Now that's popularity.

Take a hard look at this outline
of a Ford Tudor, and color it in
with your favorite colors.

Forty Ford Coupe but shown below is the Tudor with a back seat you could live in, one of the all time great HotRods and drivers.

Here's a HotRod pickup that's
not a Ford. To be sure it's a
Rod, it's a Dodge and it looks
like a great driver, fun to go
anyplace in and back. The
crank out windshield for a little
cool air on a hot summer night
sure beats air conditioning.

While we are looking at trucks, look at this useful little number. Model T Ford completely rebuilt from the suspension, chassis and box... it sports a big 383 V8, this old timer can really haul and is even more useful than a pickup. Year of origin, 1925 wow, do the math on that!

Take a close look at this HotRod, everything about this race car says HotRod but it was built by Ak Miller for the famous Carrera Pan American Road Race. It is a Race Car. '50 Ford frame topped with a T roadster body "Iron Horse" was powered by a 357 Olds, and while most HotRods spend their life in the street this was a real race car, purpose built for that race but it's still a HotRod.

The last example here is what we call a smoothie or Billet car. Everything that can be stripped off and cleaned up visually has been done, a true twenty first century HotRod, as high tech as they come with engine management and fuel injection.

High tech ultra sano clean, a twenty first century statement.

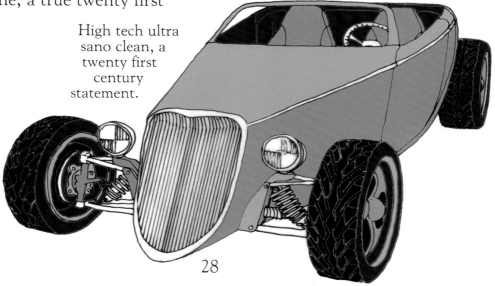

Custom cars should get a mention here because they are in a class all by themselves, as are the owners. There are exceptions but traditionally the custom builder is not at all concerned about the engine. It's usually stock untouched with the main interest being the radical alteration of the exterior, frenched headlights, nosing and decking, fender skirts, removing the chrome ornaments, chopping, cutting the top structure down to a more radical line. Chrome trim, side moldings, door handles, all gone. The grille opening modified with new and altered chrome trim in place. They are radically low to the ground many utilizing air bags and pumps to alter the height. When parked at a show some appear (and are actually) resting on the ground giving new meaning to the concept of low.

Customs are Customs not HotRods but certainly deserve a place in any special interest book of cars, they are in a class all by themselves.

A little roadster to build...

Here's a little HotRod exercise. If you found this little roadster sitting out with a For Sale sign on it, would you drag it home?

Take a hard look, it's a start and there's enough of it to see what might be. What would you do if it were up to you? Dream a little, how about an engine choice, a conservative little four banger, easy on gas and there are lots of choices, a GM Ecotec, a Quad Four or V6's, stick shift or automatic? Or would you go radical with something a little bigger? A V8 with lots of cubic inches? There are certainly plenty of choices and how would that little roadster go, it doesn't look like it weighs much.

Sooner or later every HotRodder has to make these choices, what to build? What kind and most importantly how will it be built? Traditional, Classic or right off the wall totally unexpected.

The best part of HotRods is what turns you on and the ability to dream up your own idea of what's hot and not.

30

Tractor parts on a HotRod?

Absolutely, you bet and for sure. Have a look, that grille is right off a tractor but it sure looks right sitting on the nose of that driver.

It should be clear to all that when building a HotRod anything goes... as long as it looks right and it works. The really amazing thing about that statement above is how it's arrived at. How can so many gents from so many walks of life and backgrounds quietly agree on what's right, oh and what's not.

The social aspects of the hobby are clear, groups of guys join clubs but not to fall in step with others, they join to find support and answers to difficult problems building HotRods, and believe me there are plenty. Very few gents know it all (there are a few) but someone can always be found with answers to particular questions. Electrical, carburetion, cam-shafts the list is endless and one lifetime is never long enough to really learn it all..

Before I get too far astray here, let me just say I think this little driver shows all the right attitude, right down to the tractor parts.

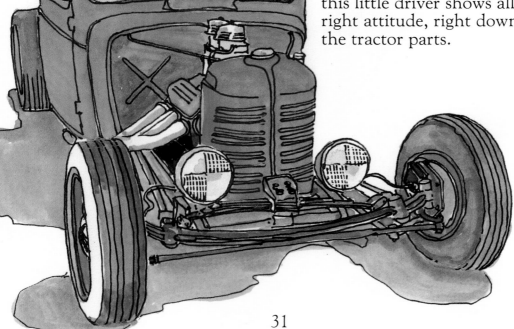

31

What is a HotRod?

I seem to recall sometime in the past hearing a story about a Supreme Court Justice who was asked to rule on what something was by definition. His response was much like what any one of us would have said, "I can't really define it but I certainly know it when I see it."

Well that goes for me as well, what's a HotRod? Well, I feel very confident that I certainly know what one is. Some weeks ago if you had showed up in a Willys Jeep Station Wagon and called it a HotRod I might have had some rude comment.

But after having a ride in a very well put together Jeep Wagon, and I mean some ride, I'd have to state it is certainly by any definition a HotRod. First, it's lowered down significantly. You can hear it coming in both exhaust note and idle attitude, kinda cammy.

The Mustang II suspension certainly improves the factory handling, and disc brakes...well, they really work. Now to my certain knowledge no HotRod has any extra room in it. But simply in terms of space this thing is a cavern. And I'll bet it can haul a troop of Boy Scouts no problem. It definitely is a HotRod.

The pickup truck Ford Motor Company never built.

Back in 1937 the Ford Motor Company introduced a daring new automobile. It followed an Art Deco design popular at the time.

The executives running Ford felt that the car design was so advanced the pickup truck buyers were going to be too conservative to accept it. Not only were the hood, grille and fenders radical for that time, for the first time the headlights were molded into the fenders. Instead, the truck got a rounded oval grille and the headlights stayed on the pedestals on top of the fenders like the previous years.

What you see here is a 1937 pickup, but with the hood, grille and fenders from the 1937 car. That is kinda what HotRodding is all about, making changes. It has been our experience that

whenever this truck shows up at a Rod Run the gents who know their old Fords are stumped because they know Ford never built it. But, it is all Ford steel, no fiberglass just thoughtful alterations that look very real.

With the usual modifications, Mustang front end, disc brakes and a small block Chevy it's pure HotRod. Oh yeah, you can hear it coming too. If you wonder what a 1937 pickup looks like have a look at page 46.

33

The last picture here represents a mind's eye
view of what's in the heart of a traditional
Hot Rodder. If you could just have a quick
look at what's going on in his head this is
what you might see, a lot of HotRod images.

Here's where we return to the engine section. Traditional and newer engines powering HotRods. Earlier we covered the early four cylinder engines and some of what was available to modify them.

The Ford, Mercury Flat Head V8 had a two decade run as a hot engine with a lot of performance parts available.

While the flat head V8s were in their last stages of development the overhead valve engines were really making their mark. In terms of horsepower, there was just no comparison.

In the fifties the major auto manufacturers were beginning to produce some serious engines, all had overhead valves, all made considerable horsepower. One of the greats that appeared in 1955 was the Chevrolet small block. Starting small at 265 cubic inches, then going to 283, 302, 327 and then the 350. What is interesting is this engine's dimensions were very close to the ubiquitous flat head.

There are lots of arguments for why this particular engine became so popular but today it's fair to say most HotRods are powered by a 350 Chevy small block. Could be that as it rapidly became the favorite more manufacturers made more specialty items for that engine and coupled with the strong reliability of the unit there's a reason for it being in nearly every rod built today. Lots of performance options at a reasonable cost.

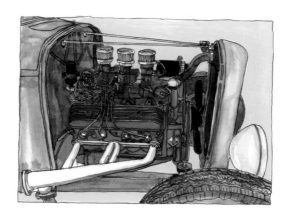

Small Block Chevy

Shown here is the Chrysler Hemi, the hemispherical combustion chambered engine with an interesting story. Every one seems to have heard the term "Hemi." Smart marketing did that. What the design of the engine did was make a very common occurrence in all engines special. Most folks think when the cylinder has taken a fresh charge of fuel and air and the spark plug ignites it there's a big bang, an explosion. Well, not really, when the spark plug ignites the mixture there is a flame front that burns from the plug outward causing immense pressure. Now if you had a completely round combustion chamber and the spark plug was at the very top and very center of that chamber when it ignites the charge it burns from point of origin in a perfectly symmetrical way pushing the piston evenly and exactly down as the flame front consumes the mixture burning out from center. Dead even combustion whereas, many of the other examples formed a wedge or other uneven flame fronts. There were examples of this design in the early years but no one put their name on it like Chrysler. Hemis make great HotRod and race car engines.

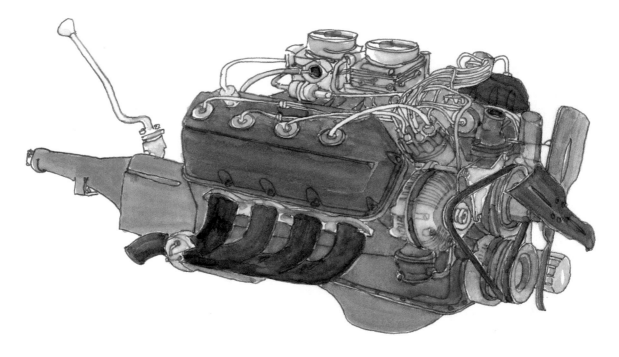

36

Supercharging
or blower motors.
In every HotRod gathering
there's always a blower or two
in attendance, jutting up
through an opening in the
hood, they do show up. Blowers
are a specially designed air pump
bolted to the top of the engine
and driven by a belt off the
front of the crank.

The concept is easier to
understand than a flame front
on a Hemi, the blower pushes
the fuel air mixture into the
engine under pressure, a lot
more pressure than the engine
could draw in on its own. The

supercharged engine shown here
probably produces more than
a thousand horsepower.

Turbo chargers work
essentially the same way but
are not powered by a belt
drive. They are motivated by
the exhaust gasses forced out
of the engine. As the exhaust
is pushed out the exhaust
manifold it spins a turbo or
small turbine which has a hot
side (exhaust) and a cold side
(intake). The hot side powers
it and the cold side is the
air pump.

37

The transmission is sometimes referred to as the gear box. That's what it is, a box of gears bolted to the back of the engine. The standard box has a shift lever so one can select the right gear for whatever driving situation is encountered. Since most engines produce power in a limited range of RPMs (revolutions per minute) getting off from stopped, or cruising down the highway, requires gear selection. As the car moves out from stopped it needs the gears changed to accommodate the movement. The faster the speed the higher the gear, the topmost being one-to-one where the engine speed and final drive speed are the same.

The automatic transmission is just that, automatic. As the car advances in speed it gets a number of signals from the engine and when needed it changes gears up and down depending on the requirements of speed of travel all by itself.

Transmissions offer great choice, what you choose depends on how you need to drive your car. Standards now come with more gears than you have fingers on one hand. Drag racers have so much power, they only have two, low and high. Automatics now even come with overdrive.

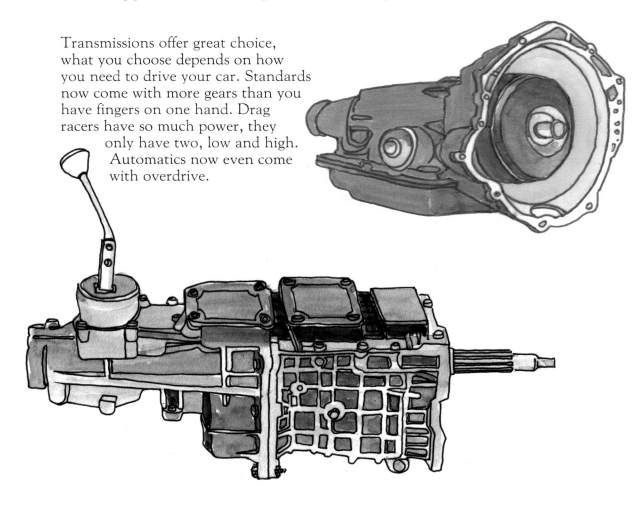

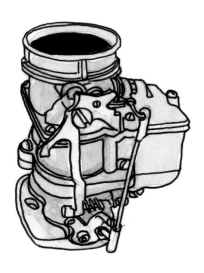

Nostalgia loves the two barrel carburetor, you can bolt a bunch of them on top or in a row, they work.

two other carbs giving a lot more performance. This was called a progressive linkage.

The other carb shown is a Quadra jet or Holley four barrel. Down the road at a reasonable rate only two barrels are functioning. Get your foot into it and the secondaries open up not unlike the multiple two barrels set up on a HotRod. In today's environment many CFM (cubic feet per minute) sized carbs are available generally ranging from 500 to 1200, depending on the need, which is the size or displacement of the engine.

The little double barrel carb shown here is from a time long past but... still used on HotRods today. Made by Stromberg or Holley and others the two barrel was a favorite. They are usually found in two's and three's in early hot rods, there are examples out there with six of them bolted to the top of an engine. The usual HotRod set up was three. When just driving around town the engine runs off the one middle carb, when some extra boost was needed the gas pedal, when depressed, open the

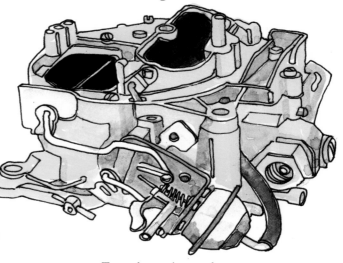

Four barrels work too but when the price of gas gets much worse everyone will be wanting fuel injection.

HotRod Chassis
1932 Ford Frame Rails
Small Block Chevy V8

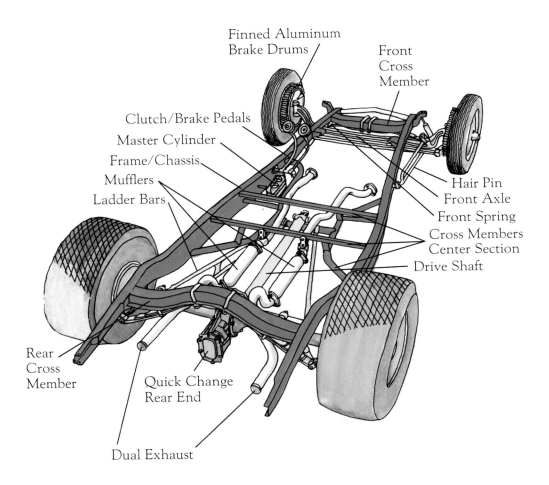

Finned Aluminum
Brake Drums

Front
Cross
Member

Clutch/Brake Pedals
Master Cylinder
Frame/Chassis
Mufflers
Ladder Bars

Hair Pin
Front Axle
Front Spring
Cross Members
Center Section
Drive Shaft

Rear
Cross
Member

Quick Change
Rear End

Dual Exhaust

A rolling chassis. Building the frame for a rod is serious stuff but very straightforward. Follow the captions and call-outs to identify the elements of a HodRod chassis. How much can you identify?

Small Block
Chevrolet V8
Installed

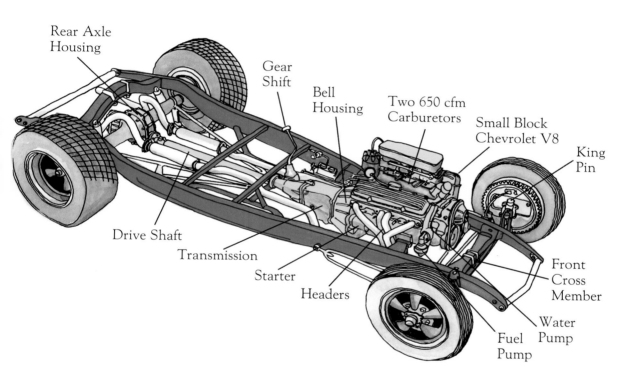

Rear Axle
Housing

Gear
Shift

Bell
Housing

Two 650 cfm
Carburetors

Small Block
Chevrolet V8

King
Pin

Drive Shaft

Transmission

Starter

Headers

Fuel
Pump

Water
Pump

Front
Cross
Member

The Dragster

In a book that looks at cars and their origins we should mention a Dragster, or a Rail Job. Either name works to describe a race car that runs only on a Drag Strip, the quarter mile, a very specialized machine.

The strip it travels on is dead straight and very smooth. There are no corners and once started no reason to ever stop as the object is to see how fast that quarter mile can be covered.

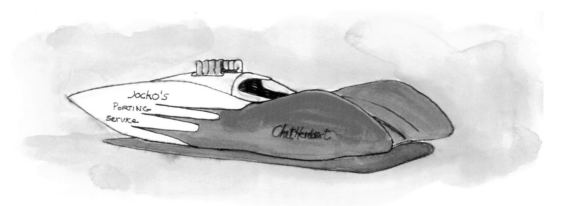

Jocko Johnson

Jocko Johnson was an Artist, he carved and sculpted metal. He had designed and built some very beautiful streamliners that he later made into handsome sculptures.

The car above and another are presently on display at the Don Garlits Museum of Drag Racing in Ocala, Florida. You should see them if you can.

42

An important consideration when building a HotRod is to build it safe. Two features to consider are a roll bar, properly constructed with a full hoop, a cross bar and struts welded to the frame. Good quality seat belts are a must and only work if buckled up!

Tools

Working on a HotRod will require some tools and good tools will last a lifetime, even if they are used a lot.

It is never really too soon to start collecting them and over the years you will certainly have your favorites. For some reason my favorite is a box end wrench 1/2" and 9/16" made about fifty years ago by Craftsman which is part of Sears. There's something about those two sizes and an old

Ford, more often than not it seemed to be what was needed.

There is no list that can be made that will have everything you will need, experience is going to be the best teacher and often the job or task you undertake will certainly tell you what you need by what you don't have. Start with a small steel tool box and start adding a little at a time. Pliers and a good screwdriver, both kinds. A set of quarter inch drive sockets, tool handles, a ratchet. Get good stuff and be selective.

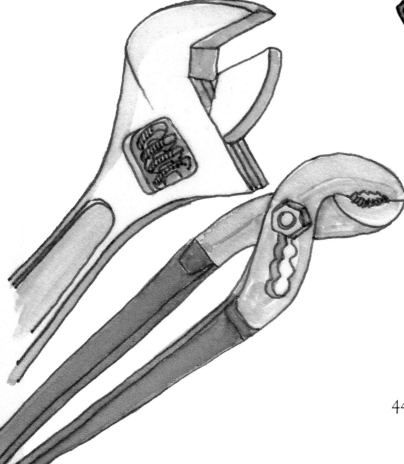

44

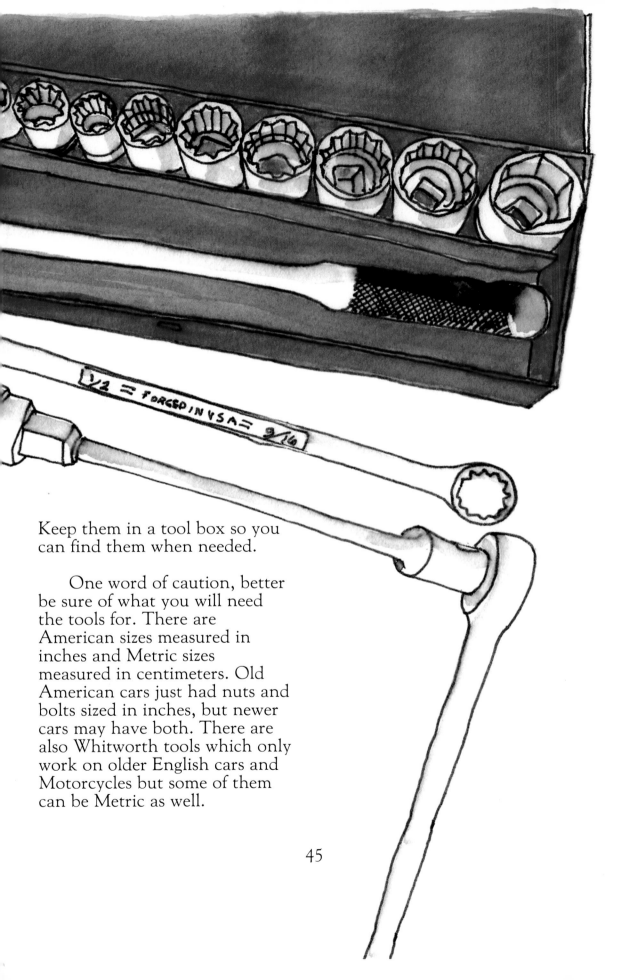

Keep them in a tool box so you can find them when needed.

One word of caution, better be sure of what you will need the tools for. There are American sizes measured in inches and Metric sizes measured in centimeters. Old American cars just had nuts and bolts sized in inches, but newer cars may have both. There are also Whitworth tools which only work on older English cars and Motorcycles but some of them can be Metric as well.

45

Model Cars and Kit Bashing

One of the great and fun ways to learn about how HotRods are put together is by making model cars. All the parts are there and they are exactly like a real car, it's amazing how much detail there is. Even choosing a color and getting it painted is a challenge but well worth the satisfaction for a job well done.

The next stage in model building is called Kit Bashing. This is where you assemble one car from two or more car kits. You have to exercise your imagination to see what is possible by combining elements from two or more cars, that is what HotRodding is all about.

I wanted to build a real pickup truck combining a truck and a sedan that Ford built in 1937. That year the car and the pick up truck were very different in appearance.

Notice how different the headlights and the grille shells are.

from the previous year's but the sedan was completely new. This was the first year the headlights were faired into the fenders. This style was called Art Deco.

What I wanted to do was combine the front fenders, grille, hood and hood sides from the sedan into the front of the truck replacing the whole nose of the truck with that of the car. This is HotRodding at it's best.

If you look closely at the two white cast plastic bodies shown you begin to see the possibilities, this could work, this could work quite well.

The front fenders are carefully cut away from the firewalls on both bodies, being careful not to cut too much off the running boards as they will support the nose when first attached.

Some attention should now be taken assembling the chassis and all the related parts. Axles, engine and transmission, drive shaft, exhaust and muffler's,

Once the cab and box are attached to the frame you can see what will have to be shaved or worked to get the car nose on the truck, a little tuck here and

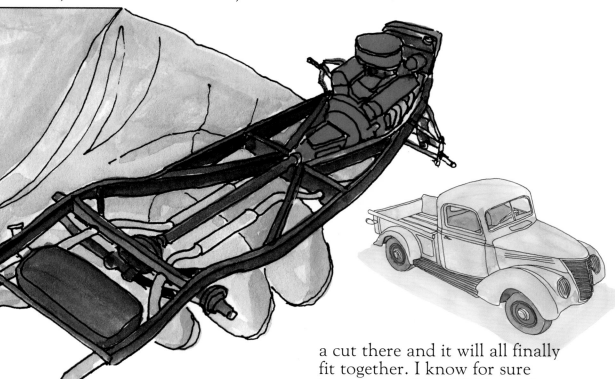

tailpipes. The chassis is the frame for the truck and everything is attached to and supported by it. What a wonderful thing to be able to hold the whole painted arrangement in the palm of your hand and see how all the parts fit together.

a cut there and it will all finally fit together. I know for sure because my friend Mike built the real thing from the model, and what is wonderful about it is all the real experts all know Ford never built a truck with the car nose on it in 37 but here it is all in original Ford factory steel. That's Hot Rodding at its best.

47

Glossary of Terms

Brakes, Basically two kinds. Drum and Disc. Drum style is an enclosed system, with brake shoes set in the rotating drum. To stop, the shoes expand gripping the inside of the drum. Disc brakes have a caliper that grabs a rotating disc to stop.

Cam, Camshaft opens and closes valves in an engine enabling it to breathe.

Carburetor, The device on an engine that mixes fuel and air for combustion. Sometimes on a HotRod more than one, as much for appearance as performance.

Chassis, The frame for a car often altered to produce better performance in handling.

Chopped Top, One of the biggest changes to a car's appearance is lowering the top. By cutting a number of inches out of the areas that support the roof, the profile of the car can be radically altered. It is rare that an older car with all its upright standing tall sheet metal escapes the cutting torch for a lower profile.

Compression Ratio, This is simply a measure of how much the piston in the cylinder compresses the fuel air mixture.

Differential, Gears in the rear axle that allow the axles (and wheels) to travel different distances around a corner.

Distributor, The engine mounted device that supplies the spark to the spark plugs firing them at the exact moment when needed.

Duals, Otherwise known as twice pipes. Dual exhausts, to relieve back pressure, are found on most HotRods, the better examples have a wonderful sound from mellow to just plain bad boy.

Fuel Injection, High pressure nozzles that mix (atomize) the fuel and air mixture much more efficiently than carburetors.

Fuel Pump, A mechanical or electric pump to carry the fuel from the gas tank to the engine.

Grille Shell, The radiator enclosure on early cars and trucks.

Hot Cam, A highly modified camshaft ground for high performance.

Lowering, Altering the chassis and suspension to lower a car for better handling and appearance.

Manifold, An arrangement of passages or pipes that allows one to feed into a number of connected pipes as in passages from one to eight or from eight into one.

Mill, a Hot Mill short hand name for engine, generally of some performance.

Quick Change, Part of the rear axle differential, a gear set that permits quick&easy gear ratio changes.

Radiator, A core with finned tubes running through it to circulate the coolant from the hot engine to allow cool air to pass through it as a heat exchanger. There is also a fan to pull the air.

Roll Bars, The best safety item you can put in a HotRod, a full overhead hoop, cross bar and struts at an angle into the trunk welded to the frame.

Seat Belts, Critical element in all cars but just having them is not enough, they have to be buckled up to be effective, use 'em!

Shocks (slang for Shock Absorbers), For every action there's a re-action. When the suspension hits a bump the car springs react and want to do a re-bound, the shock absorbers control that re-bound movement keeping everything smooth and level.

Slicks, The wide flat, treadless tires found on the back wheels of drag cars. Just about the stickiest rubber combination known to gain as much traction on acceleration as possible.

Sway Bar, A heavy steel bar that is linked to each side of the frame rails on the ends, when the car leans or sways into a turn the sway bar resists this tipping movement.

Transmission, Just like it sounds, a transmission transfers engine power (torque) through the driveshaft to the driven axle, a manual transmission must be manually shifted, each gear. An automatic transmission shifts itself when the speed is right.

49

About the American Hot Rod Foundation

The American Hot Rod Foundation was founded in 2002 by Carol, Steve and Jack Memishian to preserve the history of American hot rodding. We did it because the half-century of hot rodding before and after WWII was arguably one of the most important periods in American history: grass-roots innovation by regular guys, and an enormous and lasting impact on American culture.

Perhaps more importantly, no one but a few authors cared enough to record the personal stories of the men who built and raced amazing cars, men with no engineering degrees and little money.

Many important pioneers had already left us, so we started a race against time, recording as many of these legends as we could on network quality videotape. We also built an extensive collection of vintage photos and film. Though the work continues today 24/7, we can safely say that the history of hot rodding will never die.

If you enjoyed The Great American HotRod Explained visit our website at ahrf.com to discover more great products

DEUCE
No car in the history of hot rodding is more revered, written about and photographed than the 1932 Ford. Known as the DEUCE, this in-depth documentary is packed with celebrities, the legends of hot rodding who made the DEUCE what it is, and amazing cars. A 50 minute Digital Video DVD.

SLINGSHOT
The story of the birth of drag racing. It's a tale that fuses ingenious machines with a lifestyle lived on the edge. How California kids in the 40's and 50's transformed illegal street racing into a huge international sport today. Interviews with eighteen hot rod legends combined with lots of vintage photos and film. A 30 minute Digital Video DVD.